Questions AND Answers

DINOSAURS

Wendy Madgwick

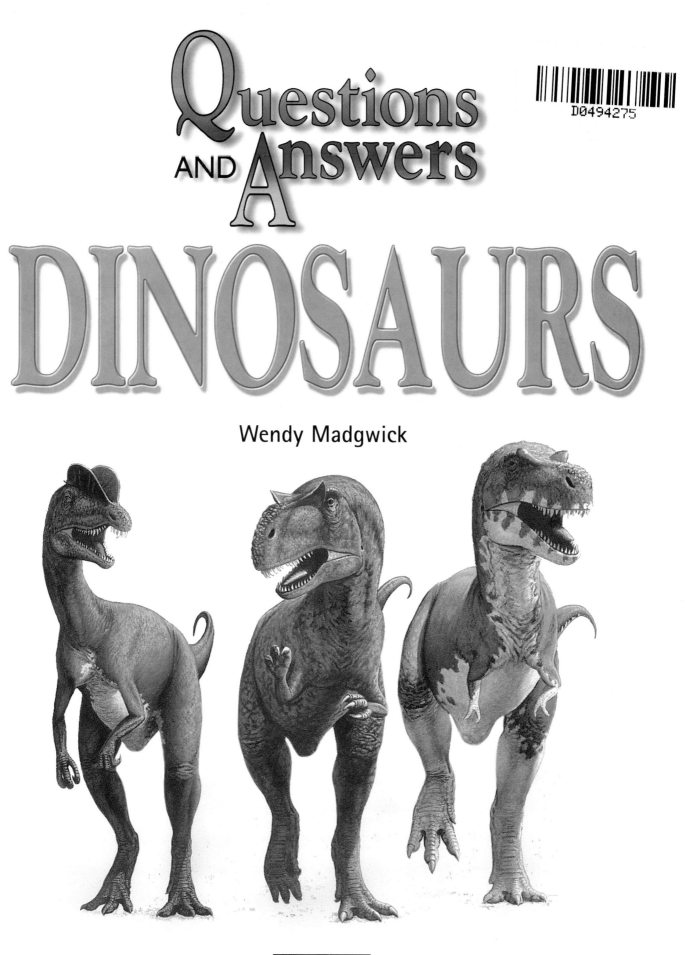

KINGfISHER

KINGFISHER
Kingfisher Publications Plc
New Penderel House
283-288 High Holborn
London WC1V 7HZ
www.kingfisherpub.com

First published by Kingfisher Publications Plc in 2000
10 9 8 7 6 5 4 3

3TR(1BCA)/1200W/TIM/HBM/130MA

Copyright © Kingfisher Publications Plc 2000

ISBN 0 7534 0479 6

Printed in China

Author: Wendy Madgwick
Designed, edited and typeset: Tucker Slingsby Ltd

Illustrations:
Marion Appleton, Richard Bonson, Jim Channel, Sandra Doyle, James Field,
Chris Forsey, Terry Gabby, Tim Hayward, Christian Hook, David Hurrel, Mark Iley,
Ian Jackson, Terence Lambert, Bernard Long, Shirley Mallinson, Robert Morton,
William Oliver, Roger Payne, Andrew Robinson, Eric Robson, Tim Slade,
Ann Winterbotham
p.12 tl courtesy of the Department Library Services, American Museum of
Natural History, Neg. no. 410 764, Shackelford 1925

Contents

Digging up the Facts

Millions of years ago dinosaurs ruled the Earth, but they died out long before people existed. We only know about dinosaurs from their fossils – animal and plant remains that have been preserved in rocks, and which we can still see today.

How are fossils dug up?

When a dinosaur fossil is found, fossil experts, called palaeontologists, carefully clear away the overlying rocks. They photograph, measure and record the position of each bone. Then the bones are dug up, wrapped in layers of paper and plaster and left to dry. This plaster 'coat' protects the fossil on its journey to the museum, where the fossil is rebuilt. Sometimes a whole dinosaur skeleton is put together in this way.

How is a fossil formed?

When an animal or plant dies, it usually rots away. However, if it is buried quickly by mud or sand, parts of it may survive. Over millions of years it will turn into a fossil.

1 A dinosaur dies and its flesh is eaten or rots away.

2 Its skeleton is covered by layers of mud or sand.

3 Slowly, mud turns to rock, and bones become fossils.

4 As the rock wears away, the fossil is revealed.

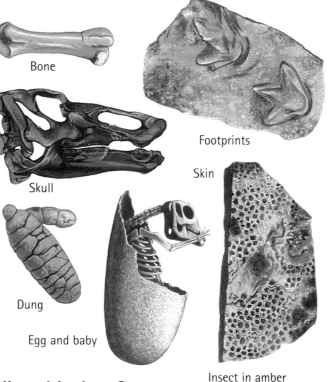

Bone

Footprints

Skull

Skin

Dung

Egg and baby

Insect in amber

What kinds of fossils are there?

Fossil bones and teeth are not the only dinosaur remains. Fossil imprints of their scaly skin, footprints and nests of eggs have all been found. Scientists can even tell what dinosaurs ate from their fossilized dung. Some fossils form in other ways. For example, an insect trapped in the sticky resin of a tree can be fossilized when the resin turns into hard amber.

Quick-fire Quiz

1. What are fossil experts called?
a) Fossiologists
b) Palaeontologists
c) Rock collectors

2. Where are most fossils found?
a) Soil
b) Wood
c) Rock

3. Who invented the word 'dinosaur'?
a) Mary Mantell
b) Edwin Cope
c) Richard Owen

4. What does *Megalosaurus* mean?
a) Fierce lizard
b) Big lizard
c) Toothed lizard

George Cuvier — Mary Mantell — Gideon Mantell — Richard Owen — Edwin Cope — Othniel Marsh

William Buckland

One name or two?

Dinosaur names are in Latin and have two parts — the genus name and the species name. They are written in italics and the genus name has a capital letter, e.g. *Tyrannosaurus rex*. Similar species of dinosaur are put in the same genus, which is the name usually used.

Who found the first dinosaur bones?

Dinosaur bones were first found hundreds of years ago, but people thought they were from giants or dragons. In 1822, Georges Cuvier suggested they belonged to giant reptiles. In 1824, William Buckland named the first dinosaur *Megalosaurus* (big lizard). A year later, fossil hunters Mary and Gideon Mantell named a second dinosaur, *Iguanodon*. Then, in 1842, Richard Owen called them 'dinosaurs', meaning 'terrible lizards'. In America over 130 new kinds of dinosaur were found by Edward Cope and Othniel Marsh.

Colour and Camouflage

No-one knows for sure what colour dinosaurs were. A few pieces of fossil dinosaur skin have been found, but the colour faded millions of years ago. Perhaps they had similar colours to reptiles today.

What use are colours?

Deinonychus

Skin colour can help animals to hide, to attract a mate or to act as a warning. Many dinosaurs were probably camouflaged. Their skins may have been patterned to blend in with their surroundings. *Deinonychus* could have been sand-coloured, like lions today, to blend in with the sandy ground or dry, yellow plants. Or perhaps *Deinonychus* were striped like tigers so that they could hide among the vegetation until the pack was ready to attack.

Saurolophus

Kritosaurus

Corythosaurus

Tsintaosaurus

Edmontosaurus

Could dinosaurs see in colour?

No-one knows for sure. We do know that some dinosaurs, called hadrosaurs, had crests, frills and inflatable air sacs on their heads. The hadrosaurs' heads and crests were probably brightly coloured so that they could be seen easily. Perhaps the dinosaurs also used their crests to send signals to each other. Several modern-day reptiles send signals in this way, so it is likely that some dinosaurs could see colours.

Striped dinosaurs?

A zebra's stripes breaks up its outline, making it hard for a predator to pick one animal out from the herd. Dinosaurs which lived in herds may have had stripes for the same reason.

Were male and female dinosaurs different colours?

Mallard ducks

It is quite possible that they were. The male and female adults of many animals today, including some birds and lizards, are very differently coloured. The male may use his bright colours to attract a female or to warn off other males. Females may have dull, drab colours so they are less easy to spot when sitting on eggs or looking after babies. When artists first started drawing dinosaurs they tended to make them all brown or green, but now dinosaurs are often shown with very colourful markings.

Collared lizards

Female

Male

Smooth or scaly?

Fossils and mummified skin show that many dinosaurs had skin covered with lumps and bumps for protection. Several colourful reptiles today have similar skins, so some experts think dinosaurs were also brightly coloured.

Parasaurolophus

Male

Female

Quick-fire Quiz

1. Which of these had a large crest?
a) *Deinonychus*
b) *Corythosaurus*
c) *Kritosaurus*

2. Why was dinosaur skin bumpy?
a) For protection
b) For warmth
c) For camouflage

3. Why might dinosaurs have had stripes?
a) To show off
b) To confuse predators
c) To attract mates

4. What is camouflage?
a) Blending in with the surroundings
b) Changing colour
c) Having bright warning colours

Dinosaur Giants

Dinosaurs are the biggest land animals that have ever lived on Earth. The largest were the plant-eating sauropods. There were several kinds and they all had enormous bodies, long necks and small heads. Some were as tall as a four-storey building.

Which is the largest complete fossil dinosaur?

The biggest almost complete skeleton found so far is that of *Brachiosaurus*. This dinosaur was so tall it could raise its head 13 metres above the ground. One *Brachiosaurus* would have weighed as much as ten large elephants.

Which was the heaviest dinosaur?

Only a few bones of *Supersaurus* and *Ultrasaurus* have been found but they both outweigh *Brachiosaurus*. *Ultrasaurus* holds the record at almost 30 metres long, 12 metres high and up to 130 tonnes in weight. That is as heavy as 20 large elephants.

Brachiosaurus

Diplodocus

Apatosaurus

The huge sauropods were many times bigger than today's largest land animal, the elephant.

Which dinosaurs had the heaviest bones?

Sauropod dinosaurs had the biggest and heaviest bones. A thigh bone weighing 450 kilograms has been found. Early fossil-hunters struggled to get their finds home. Now helicopters are often used.

Some sauropod hip bones are bigger than an adult man.

Were dinosaurs brainy?

Dinosaurs may have been big, but they were not all very bright. Most of them, like this *Stegosaurus*, had a small brain. Weight for weight, *Brachiosaurus* had the smallest brain of almost any known dinosaur. Its brain weighed only one hundred thousandth of its body weight. You are much brainier: a human brain weighs a fortieth of an adult's body weight. But fossils show us that some dinosaurs had much bigger brains and were probably quite smart.

How big did dinosaurs grow?

It is hard to work out the size of the biggest dinosaurs because only a few bones have been found. Experts think that *Ultrasaurus* was the heaviest and that *Seismosaurus* was the longest (39–52 metres). That's longer than a blue whale – the biggest animal alive today.

Blue whale

Which was the biggest carnivore?

Tyrannosaurus rex was one of the biggest meat-eating dinosaurs. It grew up to 14 metres long and over 5 metres high. Its head alone was over a metre in length. It could have opened its mouth wide enough to swallow you whole!

Which dinosaur had the biggest feet?

The front feet of sauropods such as *Brachiosaurus* were huge – up to a metre long. Some fossilized sauropod footprints are big enough to sit in. A sauropod's feet had to be big to support the dinosaur's great weight. Palaeontologists can work out an animal's size, weight and speed from its footprints.

No dinosaur could ever really have lived like this.

Did dinosaurs live under water?

No. People once thought that *Brachiosaurus* was too big to live on land. They thought it supported its weight by living in water and breathing through the nostrils on the top of its head. We now know this was not true. The pressure of the water would have crushed its ribs and stopped *Brachiosaurus* from breathing.

Quick Fire Quiz

1. How long was *Tyrannosaurus'* head?
a) Over 10m
b) Over 2m
c) Over 1m

2. Which dinosaurs lived under water?
a) None of them
b) *Stegosaurus*
c) *Brachiosaurus*

3. Which is the most complete sauropod skeleton?
a) *Brachiosaurus*
b) *Tyrannosaurus*
c) *Ultrasaurus*

4. What is the biggest animal alive today?
a) Elephant
b) *Seismosaurus*
c) Blue whale

Small Dinosaurs

Not all dinosaurs were huge. Some were as small as modern-day lizards. Fewer fossils of small dinosaurs have been found because they were often eaten by other dinosaurs and their fragile bones were easily broken.

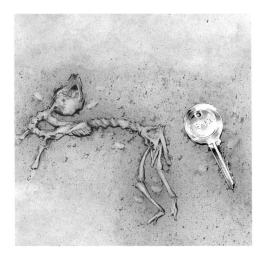

What is the smallest dinosaur skeleton?

A *Mussaurus* (mouse-lizard) skeleton found in Argentina in South America was tiny enough to fit into the palm of your hand. The skeleton was a baby dinosaur with a big head, eyes and feet. Small eggs, about 2.5 centimetres long, were found nearby. An adult *Mussaurus* would have been about 3 metres long.

What did small dinosaurs eat?

1 Some small dinosaurs ate plants, while others fed on insects, worms or small reptiles. Tiny *Lesothosaurus* lived in herds and fed on plants. It relied on speed to outrun predators.

Leaellynasaura

Which were the smallest dinosaurs?

One of the earliest and smallest meat-eating dinosaurs was *Saltopus*. At just 60 centimetres long its body was the same size as that of a large chicken. *Saltopus* was a speedy hunter and could catch fast-moving lizards and flying insects. In 1984, a small plant-eating dinosaur, *Leaellynasaura*, was found in Australia. It was about the same size as *Saltopus*. However, some scientists think that the fossils were not fully grown and that adult *Leaellynasaura* may have been up to 2 metres long.

Saltopus

2 *Compsognathus* was the size of a large pet cat. It moved quickly, using its speed to catch fast-moving prey like insects and lizards. One fossil *Compsognathus* skeleton has been found with the remains of its last meal, a lizard, inside it.

3 *Hypsilophodon* was a speedy little dinosaur that grew to about 2 metres long. It lived in forests and used its horny beak to nip off juicy shoots from plants.

4 Wolf-sized *Oviraptor* may have darted along at up to 50 kilometres an hour. It hunted lizards and small mammals and raided other dinosaurs' nests to snatch the eggs.

How big were dinosaur babies?

Newly hatched dinosaur babies were very small. You could have held this baby *Protoceratops* in your hand. One baby *Troodon* fossil has been found that is only 7 centimetres long — the size of a large hen's egg.

Did small dinosaurs defend themselves?

Scutellosaurus was only the size of a cat, but this little plant-eater was no easy meal for big dinosaurs. It was protected by rows of small bony knobs along its back and tail, and was the smallest armour-plated dinosaur.

Dinosaur Babies

Less than 100 years ago, scientists were not sure how dinosaur babies were born. In 1923, an expedition to the Gobi Desert in Mongolia found a nest of fossilized dinosaur eggs, laid over 100 million years earlier. This proved that dinosaurs laid eggs on land.

Who found the first eggs?

Roy Chapman Andrews discovered the first dinosaur eggs in 1923 in the Gobi Desert. He worked for the American Museum of Natural History and led many exciting dinosaur-hunting expeditions. He even used specially adapted cars to drive across the Gobi desert. Some people think he was the original 'Indiana Jones'.

How big were dinosaurs' eggs?

Dinosaur eggs were laid in clutches of ten to 40. Their size varied according to the size of the adult, but the eggs were small for such large animals. For example, a 30-metre long female probably laid eggs about 60 centimetres long. A really huge egg was not possible because it would need such a thick shell the baby could not break out of it.

Some dinosaur eggs had rough shells and others had smooth.

Did dinosaurs build nests?

1 Some dinosaurs, such as the *Maiasaura*, certainly built nests. *Maiasaura* lived in herds. Every year the females gathered at the same nesting site. We know this because a huge nesting area has been found in Montana, United States.

Did dinosaurs look after their babies?

Experts think that some kinds of baby dinosaurs, such as young *Maiasaura*, were not very well developed. The adults probably fed their newly hatched young on soft plant shoots until they were able to fend for themselves. The babies of other dinosaurs, such as *Orodromeus*, were well developed and could probably run soon after they hatched. So perhaps, like many reptiles today, these dinosaurs laid lots of eggs and left their hatchlings to look after themselves.

2 Female *Maiasaura* made a low mound of mud about 2 metres across. Each female dug out a nest and lined it with twigs and leaves.

Did dinosaurs egg sit?

In 1993, 70 years after Roy Chapman Andrews found the first dinosaur eggs, another expedition set out for the Gobi Desert. This time, the scientists discovered the fossilized remains of an *Oviraptor* sitting on a nest of eggs. The find proved that some kinds of dinosaurs sat on their eggs to hatch them, in the same way that birds do today.

Quick-fire Quiz

1. **Where were the first eggs found?**
a) Sahara Desert
b) Gobi Desert
c) Kalahari Desert

2. **Which dinosaur stole eggs?**
a) *Troodon*
b) *Triceratops*
c) *Maiasaura*

3. **Who found the first eggs?**
a) Indiana Jones
b) Richard Owen
c) Roy Chapman Andrews

4. **What were *Maiasaura* nests made of?**
a) Stones
b) Mud
c) Paper

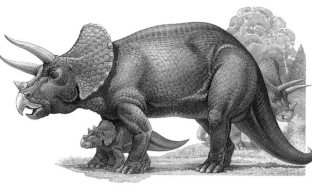

Did dinosaurs defend their young?

Armoured dinosaurs like *Triceratops* may have defended their young by charging a would-be predator. Scientists think a herd of adult plant-eaters on the move defended their young by keeping them in the middle of the herd.

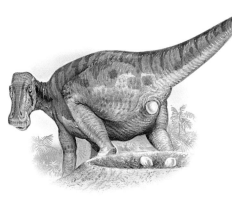

3 Each female laid about 20 to 25 eggs in the nest. She covered them with more plants to keep them warm.

4 The *Maiasaura* mother guarded her eggs carefully. Egg-thieves, such as *Troodon*, were always ready to snatch an easy meal.

5 The *Maiasaura* hatchlings broke out of their egg shells using a special sharp tooth on their snouts.

Communication

Animals cannot talk to each other, so they communicate in other ways. They use sounds, smells, touch and visual signals to tell each other what is going on. Dinosaurs may have used similar methods to send 'messages' to one another.

Why was making a noise useful?

Dinosaurs may have used sound to warn of danger or keep in touch with other members of a large herd. *Parasaurolophus* may have hooted a warning if danger threatened. The duck-billed dinosaur *Edmontosaurus* may have blown up a bag of skin over its nose and bellowed loudly at rival males. Young dinosaurs may have squeaked to get an adult's attention.

What sounds did dinosaurs make?

Dinosaurs had complex ears and could probably hear well, so they may have used many different sounds to send signals to each other. Like reptiles alive today, most dinosaurs could probably hiss or grunt and large ones may have roared. A few, like the hadrosaurs, probably made distinctive calls to each other through their horns, crests and inflatable nose flaps. Scientists believe this is possible because, when they blew through models of different hadrosaur skulls, they found that each skull gave a different sound.

Tsintaosaurus

Edmontosaurus

Lambeosaurus

Corythosaurus

Male peacock displaying

Did dinosaurs display like birds?

Experts think that some male dinosaurs displayed to the females during the mating season. Just as peacocks display their coloured feathers, male dinosaurs may have displayed bright head crests, spines or neck ruffs to attract females and warn off rival males.

Did dinosaurs use their noses?

Fossils of dinosaurs' brains suggest that many dinosaurs had a good sense of smell and most dinosaurs had well-developed nostrils. A strong sense of smell would have helped dinosaurs sniff out food. If, as some scientists think, dinosaurs gave off scent signals, they may also have used their sense of smell to find a mate. *Brachiosaurus* had huge nostrils on the top of its head. No-one knows why, but perhaps they allowed it to eat water plants and breathe at the same time.

Brachiosaurus

Parasaurolophus herd

Quick-fire Quiz

1. Which dinosaur group had head crests?
   a) Hadrosaurs
   b) Theropods
   c) Lizards

2. Which dinosaur had an inflatable nose flap?
   a) *Edmontosaurus*
   b) *Brachiosaurus*
   c) *Lambeosaurus*

3. Which dinosaur had a hollow crest?
   a) *Tyrannosaurus*
   b) *Brachiosaurus*
   c) *Parasaurolophus*

4. Where were *Brachiosaurus'* nostrils?
   a) On the end of its nose
   b) It didn't have any
   c) On top of its head

How did noisy noses work?

Hadrosaurs such as *Parasaurolophus* and *Lambeosaurus* had hollow crests. Air passages extended from the nose through the crest and down into the throat. The dinosaurs could hoot and honk as they breathed in and out. Different types of crest produced different notes.

Skulls

Parasaurolophus   *Lambeosaurus*

Could dinosaurs taste their food?

Many dinosaurs had tongues and they could probably taste and smell their food, like most animals today. Reptiles such as snakes use their forked tongue to 'taste' the air for traces of prey. But there is no evidence to suggest that any dinosaurs had tongues that could do this.

Plant-Eaters

Most dinosaurs were herbivores. This means they ate plants not meat. Plant-eating dinosaurs came in all shapes and sizes from small two-legged dinosaurs to huge sauropods. Plants are hard to digest so, to get enough energy from their food, many spent most of the day eating.

Lizard or bird hips?

Experts divide dinosaurs into two groups by the shape of their hips. Sauropod plant-eaters

1

(1) had lizard hips. Their big stomachs unbalanced them so they had to walk on four legs. Two-legged theropod meat-eaters

2

(2) also had lizard hips. Plant-eating bird-hipped dinosaurs

3

(3) evolved later. Many walked on two legs with their big stomach slung between their back legs. Armoured bird-hipped plant-eaters were so heavy that they walked on four legs.

Psittacosaurus

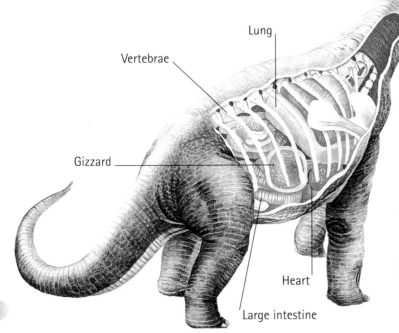

Lung

Vertebrae

Gizzard

Heart

Large intestine

Did dinosaurs eat leaves?

Leaves were the main diet of many plant-eaters. *Psittacosaurus* probably snipped leaves off with its bird-like beak, then sliced them into smaller bits with its scissor-like teeth. Like the giraffe, *Brachiosaurus* used its long neck to graze on leafy treetops.

Why were sauropods so big?

A sauropod's huge body was filled almost entirely with its guts. Sauropods like *Brachiosaurus* ate up to 200 kilograms of plants a day, so they needed a big stomach and long intestines to digest this tough food. Until recently, experts had to guess what a dinosaur's insides looked like, but in 1998 two dinosaurs from China were found with their guts intact. These should tell us more about what dinosaurs ate.

Lufengosaurus

1   2   3   4   5

Did plant–eaters have teeth?

Most plant-eating dinosaurs had teeth, and experts can tell what food a dinosaur ate by looking at these. *Lufengosaurus*, an early sauropod, had many small peg-like teeth with jagged edges. These were great for nipping off soft leaves, but no use for chewing, so *Lufengosaurus* swallowed its food whole.

Why were teeth different shapes?

The size and shape of a dinosaur's teeth depended on what it ate. The ornithopod *Heterodontosaurus* had sharp, narrow front teeth (1) for cutting and slicing. *Plateosaurus* (2) and sauropods like *Diplodocus* (3) and *Apatosaurus* (4) had peg-like teeth to shred and crush food. *Stegosaurus* (5) had leaf-shaped teeth for slicing and munching soft plants.

Why did dinosaurs swallow stones?

Small stones have been found in the rib cages of many dinosaurs. Few dinosaurs could move their jaws from side to side, so they could not chew their food. They swallowed it whole and probably swallowed small stones (gastroliths) to help them grind food as it churned about in their stomachs. Chickens swallow grit to do the same thing.

Shunosaurus

Quick-fire Quiz

1. What are gastroliths?
a) Grinding teeth
b) Stomach stones
c) Plants

2. Which dinosaur had leaf-shaped teeth?
a) *Diplodocus*
b) *Apatosaurus*
c) *Stegosaurus*

3. Which dinosaur had a bird-like beak?
a) *Shunosaurus*
b) *Brachiosaurus*
c) *Psittacosaurus*

4. What did *Triceratops* eat?
a) Fruit and nuts
b) Ferns and horsetails
c) Grass

Did dinosaurs eat grass?

Grasses did not develop on Earth until 25 million years after the dinosaurs died out. Instead, herbivorous dinosaurs ate other plants that were around at the time. Long-necked sauropods such as *Shunosaurus* used their simple peg-like teeth to munch on leaves, pine needles and juicy shoots. A hadrosaur such as *Saurolophus* ate leaves from flowering plants and crunchy pine cones. It chopped off the leaves with its horny beak, then chewed them with its flat back teeth. Horned dinosaurs like *Triceratops* sliced up tough ferns and horsetails with their sharp beaks and teeth.

Leaves, pine needles and shoots

Pine cones and shrub leaves

Ferns and horsetails

Saurolophus

Triceratops

Meat-Eaters

All meat-eating, or carnivorous, dinosaurs were theropods. (Theropod means 'beast foot'.) They walked on two legs and their three toes were armed with sharp claws. Some were fierce hunters, chasing and killing their prey. Others were scavengers, feeding on dead animals.

Did dinosaurs have sharp teeth?
The sharp, backward pointing teeth of *Megalosaurus* are typical of many large meat-eating dinosaurs. They were good for gripping and ripping their prey. Other carnivorous dinosaurs had small sharp teeth or crushing beaks.

Deinonychus   Owl

Did meat-eaters have sharp eyesight?
Many hunters such as *Deinonychus* had good eyesight. It may have had forward-facing eyes and good binocular (overlapping) vision like modern owls. This would have given it a single view of its prey and helped it judge distances.

Did all meat-eaters look the same?
Meat-eating dinosaurs came in all shapes and sizes. They ranged in size from chicken-sized *Saltopus* (60 centimetres) to huge *Tyrannosaurus* (12 metres long). Big theropods like *Tyrannosaurus*, *Allosaurus* and *Dilophosaurus* hunted large plant-eaters, while speedy *Troodon* killed small reptiles and mammals. *Struthiomimus*, *Avimimus* and *Oviraptor* used their strong beaks to catch and crush insects and eggs.

Tyrannosaurus

Troodon

Allosaurus

Avimimus

Oviraptor

Dilophosaurus

Struthiomimus

Did dinosaurs eat fish?

Experts believe that dinosaurs such as *Baryonyx* snapped up fish with their long crocodile-like jaws. *Baryonyx* may also have speared fish with the huge hook-like claw on its front feet, just as brown bears do today.

Which dinosaurs used claws to kill?

Deinonychus ('terrible claw') and its relatives specialized in using their claws to kill animals much larger than themselves. *Deinonychus* leapt at its victims, slashing them with the deadly 12 centimetres long claw on the second toe of its back foot.

Did dinosaurs hunt in packs?

Like today's wolves, some small meat-eating dinosaurs, such as *Deinonychus*, hunted in packs. This would have allowed them to hunt larger prey such as a young *Diplodocus*, separating it from the rest of its herd.

Wolf pack

Were any dinosaurs cannibals?

Fossil remains of *Coelophysis* found in New Mexico, United States, had skeletons of young ones inside them. The bones were too big to belong to unborn *Coelophysis*. Experts believe that adult *Coelophysis* would eat young of their own kind if food was short. Other dinosaurs may have been cannibals, too.

Did dinosaurs eat eggs?

Small speedy meat-eaters such as *Troodon* would snatch unguarded eggs from other dinosaurs' nests. Eggs were a good source of food — a complete meal in a shell! *Troodon* could sprint at about 50 kilometres an hour, so few lumbering plant-eaters could catch it.

19

The Fiercest Dinosaur

Tyrannosaurus rex ('king tyrant lizard') lived about 70 million years ago. At over 12 metres long and three times as tall as a man, it was one of the largest and deadliest creatures that has ever lived on land.

Has a whole *Tyrannosaurus* skeleton ever been found?

Complete fossil skeletons are very rare, but in 1990 two almost complete *Tyrannosaurus* skeletons were found in America. Experts studying these and other *Tyrannosaurus* skeletons believe that, unlike meat-eaters of today such as lions and tigers, the female *Tyrannosaurus* was probably bigger than the male.

Did *Tyrannosaurus* grasp prey with its front legs?

Tyrannosaurus' arms and hands were too small to grasp its prey. They couldn't even reach its mouth. Its head and teeth were so strong and deadly that it did not need its arms to catch its prey.

Tyrannosaurus skeleton

Dilophosaurus

Allosaurus

Albertosaurus

Were there other big meat-eaters?

These three meat-eaters were related to *Tyrannosaurus*, but were not as big. Two huge, 2.6-metre long fossil arms with clawed hands were found in Mongolia and named *Deinocheirus* ('terrible hand'). They may be from a version of *Deinonychus* that was even bigger than *Tyrannosaurus*.

How big were *T rex* teeth?

Tyrannosaurus had teeth up to 18 centimetres long. These teeth had a razor-sharp point to stab prey, and rough, saw-like edges to rip through flesh. An adult had between 50 and 100 teeth and if one fell out, it simply grew another!

Quick-fire Quiz

1. How long ago did *Tyrannosaurus* live?
a) 200 million years
b) 70 million years
c) 150 million years

2. How long were its teeth?
a) Up to 5cm
b) Up to 30cm
c) Up to 18cm

3. Which dinosaur was related to *Tyrannosaurus*?
a) *Triceratops*
b) *Albertosaurus*
c) *Deinocheirus*

4. What does *Tyrannosaurus rex* mean?
a) Big bad lizard
b) King tyrant lizard
c) Emperor reptile

Was *Tyrannosaurus* fast or slow?

Experts used to think that *Tyrannosaurus* stood upright and lumbered along, dragging its tail on the ground. By studying the more complete skeletons, they now think it leaned forward, with its tail sticking out as a balance, and that it could run fast. Judging from its skull and the size of its brain, experts think it also had good eyesight and hearing and an excellent sense of smell.

Wrong   Right

Was the fiercest dinosaur a scavenger?

Some experts think *Tyrannosaurus* was a scavenger that ate dead animals and stole prey from other predators. Others think it could run as fast as a racehorse (50 kilometres an hour) and was a fierce hunter. The latest finds show it probably did both.

Attack and Defence

Meat-eating dinosaurs were built to kill, attacking their victims with sharp teeth and slashing claws. Plant-eaters defended themselves in many different ways. Some lived in herds, some relied on speed to escape, while others developed armour and horns for fighting off enemies.

Did huge sauropods fight?

Like elephants today, the giant sauropods mostly relied on their size to protect them. Some, like *Diplodocus*, could lash their long, whip-like tails to frighten off attackers.

Which dinosaurs had armour?

Plant-eating ankylosaurs protected themselves with armour-like skin and bony spikes. *Ankylosaurus* was the size of a tank. If attacked, it crouched down to protect its soft belly and lashed out with the bony club on the end of its tail.

What use were plates and spikes?

Stegosaurus was well protected from its enemies with huge bony plates along its back and four long, sharp spikes on its thick tail. A blow from its tail could seriously injure, or even kill, an attacker.

Armour or radiators?

The plates along the back of *Stegosaurus* were covered with skin and had lots of blood vessels in them. Some experts think they may have helped the dinosaur warm its body when it basked in the sun, and to cool down by losing heat quickly in the shade. Other scientists think the plates were armour to protect it from carnosaurs (meat-eating dinosaurs such as *Tyrannosaurus*).

Did plant-eaters have claws?

Most didn't but the plant-eater *Iguanodon* had two sharp thumb spikes. Perhaps it used them to stab attackers. Or maybe the males used them to fight each other.

Which dinosaurs had horns?

Some plant-eating dinosaurs, called ceratopians, developed horns and bony frills to protect themselves. They may have charged at enemies like a rhinoceros, or maybe rival males fought by locking horns.

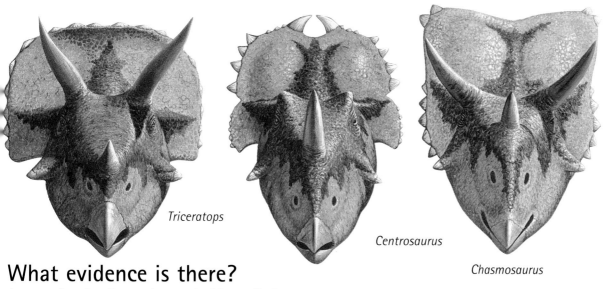

Triceratops

Centrosaurus

Chasmosaurus

What evidence is there?

An amazing fossil was dug up in Mongolia in 1971. A *Protoceratops* had charged a fierce *Velociraptor* like a rhino, smashing into it with its bony beak. The *Velociraptor's* sharp claws had pierced the stomach and throat of the *Protoceratops*. Neither survived.

Which dinosaur used its head?

Pachycephalosaurus males had very thick tops to their skulls. Rival males may have had head-butting contests to win a mate, just as some wild sheep do today.

Quick-fire Quiz

1. Which dinosaur had plates and spikes?
   a) *Stegosaurus*
   b) *Diplodocus*
   c) *Tyrannosaurus*

2. Which dinosaur had a tail club?
   a) *Velociraptor*
   b) *Ankylosaurus*
   c) *Diplodocus*

3. How did *Iguanodon* protect itself?
   a) With armour
   b) With thumb spikes
   c) With its horns

4. Which dinosaur died fighting with a *Velociraptor*?
   a) *Diplodocus*
   b) *Stegosaurus*
   c) *Protoceratops*

All Over the World

Maiasaura

Stegosaurus

This map shows where dinosaur fossils have been found. Experts have divided the dinosaur age into three main parts – the Triassic, Jurassic and Cretaceous Periods. Different dinosaurs lived in each of these periods, so some fossils are older than others.

Deinonychus

Diplodocus

What dinosaurs have been found in North America?

Hundreds of fossil dinosaurs, including *Diplodocus*, *Deinonychus* and *Stegosaurus*, have been found in North America. The famous *Tyrannosaurus* and *Triceratops* have been found only there, and nowhere else.

Cretaceous

Jurassic

Triassic

What was the fiercest dinosaur in South America?

The biggest South American meat-eater found so far is *Piatnitzkysaurus*, which was about 6 metres long and 3 metres high. It chased and killed prey in the same way as its bigger North American relative, *Allosaurus*.

Piatnitzkysaurus

Did some dinosaurs live all over the world?

Some dinosaurs, such as *Brachiosaurus*, have been found in North America, Africa and Europe. Other dinosaurs have only been found on one continent.

24

Iguanodon

Camptosaurus

Megalosaurus

Oviraptor

Protoceratops

Shantungosaurus

Kentrosaurus

Tuatara

Elaphrosaurus

Which was the first dinosaur to be named in Europe?

Megalosaurus ('great reptile'), a fierce meat-eater, was named in 1824. Since then hundreds of fossil dinosaurs have been found in Europe, including large plant-eaters such as *Camptosaurus* and *Iguanodon* which have also been unearthed in North America.

Which dinosaurs lived in Asia?

Hundreds of dinosaur remains have been found throughout Asia. The wolf-sized *Oviraptor*, was found in the remote Gobi Desert in Mongolia. *Shantungosaurus*, a duck-billed dinosaur about 12 metres tall, comes from China.

Have fossils been found in Australia?

Few dinosaur fossils have been found in Australia, but thousands of fossil dinosaur footprints were uncovered in Queensland. The most complete dinosaur find is an iguanodon, *Muttaburrasaurus*. Only one dinosaur fossil has been found in New Zealand, but the tuatara, a reptile that lives there today, looks almost exactly the same as its ancestors that lived in the dinosaur age.

Which is the biggest fossil site in Africa?

One of the biggest fossil sites in Africa is Tendaguru in Tanzania. Over 200 tonnes of dinosaur bones were found there between 1909 and 1912. Many dinosaurs were dug up, including the stegosaur *Kentrosaurus* and the small bird-like *Elaphrosaurus*.

Quick-fire Quiz

1. What is Tendaguru?
a) A city
b) A fossil site
c) A type of dinosaur

2. Which was the first dinosaur to be named in Europe?
a) *Velociraptor*
b) *Megalosaurus*
c) *Iguanodon*

3. How tall is *Shantungosaurus*?
a) About 50m
b) About 12m
c) About 5m

4. Where does the tuatara live?
a) North America
b) Australia
c) New Zealand

Living in Herds

Clues, such as footprints and the mass dinosaur graves, show that some dinosaurs lived in groups. Plant-eating dinosaurs probably herded together for safety, like antelopes do today. Some meat-eaters may have hunted in packs.

Which dinosaurs probably lived alone?

Large meat-eating dinosaurs such as *Albertosaurus* were excellent hunters and had few enemies. They could have lived and hunted alone, just as tigers do today. However, the bones of 40 young and adult *Allosaurus* were discovered in a mass grave in the United States, so perhaps they hunted in packs like lions.

Why did dinosaurs live together?

Many plant-eaters like these *Edmontosaurus* hadrosaurs lived in herds for protection. Lots of pairs of eyes keeping watch for a predator are better than one pair. It is also more difficult for a predator to attack a large moving herd. These hadrosaurs probably hooted and honked to signal to each other if there was danger, such as a carnosaur, nearby.

Did herd members look after each other?

Fossil footprints show some dinosaur herds travelled with their young in the middle and the adults on the outside. If attacked, horned dinosaurs like *Triceratops* may have formed a circle round their young, with their horns pointing out towards the enemy, as musk oxen do today.

How do we know about dinosaur herds?

Vast tracks of fossilized dinosaur footprints all going the same way were discovered in North America. Experts believe they belonged to herds of dinosaurs. Huge numbers of dinosaurs have also been found buried together. One of these burial sites contained 10,000 duck-billed *Maiasaura*. This evidence shows sauropods probably lived in groups.

Why did some herds die together?

In 1947, the fossil remains of a large herd of *Coelophysis* were found at Ghost Ranch in New Mexico in the United States. The bones came from young and old animals. Some experts think they probably all died together in a flash flood. Their bodies were carried along by the water and eventually dumped in a heap on a sandbank where they fossilized.

Did herds migrate?

Fossil dinosaurs have been found in the Arctic and Antarctic. There would have been plenty of food in the summer but little in winter. Experts think that dinosaur herds migrated away from the Poles in the winter, as modern-day caribou do.

Did dinosaurs travel far?

Like many animals today, such as caribou and wildebeest, some dinosaurs, such as these iguanodons, probably travelled huge distances in search of food.

Did dinosaur herds have look outs?

No-one knows for sure, but in large herds of animals some adults keep watch for predators. Dinosaurs probably did the same.

Which dinosaurs hunted in packs?

Carnivores like wolves and hyenas hunt in packs. Many small meat-eating dinosaurs, such as *Elaphrosaurus*, probably hunted in packs too. This would have allowed them to hunt and kill larger prey than if they hunted alone.

Fast and Slow

A dinosaur's shape, size, and the speed at which it moved, was determined by how it lived. Hunters had to be fast to catch their prey. They ran on strong back legs, using their tails to balance. Huge plant-eaters could only move slowly. They did not need to chase food and their huge size kept them safe.

Iguanodon

Megalosaurus

How can we measure a dinosaur's speed?

Experts work out the speed a dinosaur moved from the space between its footprints and the length of its legs. The wider apart a dinosaur's tracks are, the faster it was moving. If the footprints are close together, it was probably walking slowly.

Which was the fastest dinosaur?

Ostrich-sized *Struthiomimus* was one of the fastest. It had no armour or horns to protect it and had to rely on speed to escape. It was as fast as a racehorse, reaching speeds of over 50 kilometres an hour.

What can footprints tell us?

Fossilized footprints can show how dinosaurs moved. *Iguanodon* walked on all fours, but could run on its back legs. The huge three-toed prints of *Megalosaurus* show that it was a meat-eater and always moved on its back legs.

How fast did dinosaurs move?

1 Just like animals today, dinosaurs moved at different speeds at different times. *Tyrannosaurus* walked at 16 kilometres an hour but ran much faster when attacking.

2 *Hypsilophodon* was one of the speediest dinosaurs. This plant-eater could race along the ground at up to 50 kilometres an hour to escape from enemies.

3 *Apatosaurus* weighed 40 tonnes – as much as seven elephants. It walked at 10 to 16 kilometres an hour. If it had tried to run, the impact would have broken its legs.

4 *Triceratops* weighed as much as five rhinos and could also charge like a rhino at speeds of over 25 kilometres an hour. Few predators would risk attacking it.

Quick-fire Quiz

1. **How fast could *Triceratops* charge?**
a) Over 50km/hr
b) Over 25km/hr
c) Over 5km/hr

2. **Which dinosaur could reach over 50km an hour?**
a) *Apatosaurus*
b) *Struthiomimus*
c) *Brachiosaurus*

3. **Which of these show how fast dinosaurs moved?**
a) Their heads
b) Their footprints
c) Their tails

4. **Which legs did *Megalosaurus* use?**
a) Its front legs
b) All four legs
c) Its back legs

Which was the slowest dinosaur?

The huge sauropods like *Brachiosaurus* were the slowest moving dinosaurs. At over 50 tonnes, they were too heavy to run and so plodded along at about 10 kilometres an hour. Unlike smaller dinosaurs, these huge creatures were probably too big ever to have reared up on their hind legs.

Warm or cold blood?

Mammals and birds are warm-blooded – they make their own body heat. Reptiles are cold-blooded and have to warm up in the sun. To give them the energy to heat their bodies, warm-blooded animals need about ten times more food than a cold-blooded animal of the same size. Studying how much dinosaurs ate may show if any were warm-blooded.

In the Sea

While dinosaurs ruled the land, other giant reptiles took over the seas. Mosasaurs, plesiosaurs and pliosaurs were fierce predators, snapping up fish and other sea creatures. Giant turtles and crocodiles also hunted in prehistoric oceans.

Are all prehistoric sea reptiles extinct?

Most kinds of large sea reptiles died out with the dinosaurs, but turtles and crocodiles still exist. Prehistoric *Deinosuchus*, a 16-metre long crocodile, was, however, much bigger than any crocodile living today.

Deinosuchus

Kronosaurus

Mosasaurus

Teleosaurus

What did sea reptiles eat?

Sea reptiles ate fish, shellfish and even each other! A *placodont* picked up shellfish with its long front teeth. It crushed them with its back teeth, spat out the shells and swallowed the rest.

Ammonite
(swimming
shellfish)

Placodont

Why is Mary Anning famous?

Mary Anning was born in 1799 in Dorset, England. She grew up to be a great fossil hunter and was so good that she earned her living by selling fossils. She found the first complete fossil skeleton of a giant marine ichthyosaur when she was only 12 years old. Another of her amazing finds was the first complete skeleton of a plesiosaur.

Elasmosaurus

Tanystropheus

Did sea reptiles have teeth?

Most sea reptiles had large jaws full of sharp teeth to spear slippery fish or break open tough shells.

Ichthyosaurus

Did any sea creatures come on to the land?

Long-necked *Tanystropheus* hunted on both land and in the sea. It snapped up flying insects as well as slippery fish. Most sea reptiles had to come on land to lay their eggs.

How did prehistoric sea reptiles swim?

Pliosaurs like Kronosaurus and plesiosaurs like Elasmosaurus had four strong paddles instead of feet. They moved them up and down to 'fly' through the sea in the same way penguins do today. Mosasaurus, Ichthyosaurus and crocodiles such as Teleosaurus swam by beating their tails from side to side. Sea reptiles could not breathe under water, so they had to come to the surface to gulp in air.

Kronosaurus skeleton

How big were the sea reptiles?

One of the biggest sea reptiles was the pliosaur *Kronosaurus*. It was nearly 17 metres long with a huge head the size of a car. *Mosasaurus* was 10 metres long, the largest lizard ever. Prehistoric turtles were much bigger than their modern relatives. The largest, *Archelon*, was almost 4 metres long. Its huge front paddles powered it through the water at up to 15 kilometres an hour.

Archelon

Did sea reptiles lay eggs?

Most sea reptiles laid their eggs on land, like turtles today. But *Ichthyosaurus* gave birth to live young in the same way as sea mammals like this dolphin do today.

In the Air

When dinosaurs took over the land, other reptiles took to the air. The first reptiles to become masters of flight were the pterosaurs. They ruled the skies for 166 million years but died out at the end of the dinosaur age.

How big were pterosaurs?

Pterosaurs came in many sizes. *Quetzalcoatlus* was the biggest. It had a human-sized body and a wingspan of over 12 metres — bigger than a hang glider! *Rhamphorhynchus* was the size of a crow with a wingspan of 40 centimetres.

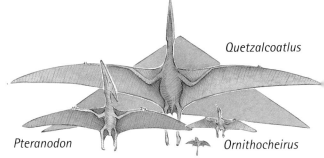

Quetzalcoatlus

Pteranodon

Ornithocheirus

Rhamphorhynchus

What did pterosaurs eat?

Pterosaurs' jaws and teeth help show what they ate. Most fed on fish, while some snapped up insects. *Pterodaustro* may have filtered tiny animals from the water with its sieve-like bottom jaw. *Dzungaripterus'* pincer-like beak could prise shellfish from rocks. *Dimorphodon*'s strong jaws were ideal for catching fish.

Pterodaustro

Dzungaripterus

Dimorphodon

Pteranodon

Did pterosaurs build nests?

No-one knows, but scientists think pterosaurs probably laid eggs. They may have laid these in nests, and sat on them to keep them warm. Fossils show that baby pterosaurs were not well developed, so perhaps the adults fed them, as baby birds are fed today.

Furry and active?

Fossil evidence shows that some pterosaurs were covered with fur, which probably means they were warm-blooded like birds. They also had big brains with large areas to control balance and sight.

When did reptiles first fly?

Reptiles first took to the air about 250 million years ago. Early flying reptiles, such as *Coelurosauravus*, were lizard-shaped with four legs. Their wings grew out from the sides of their body and were held rigid on long ribs. These reptiles used their wings to help them glide from tree to tree, but they could not flap them. One of the earliest gliding reptiles, *Longisquama*, had tall crests along its back. The crests may have opened out like wings to help it glide.

Longisquama

Coelurosauravus

Quetzalcoatlus

Bat

Did pterosaurs have tails?

All pterosaurs had tails. Early kinds, such as *Dimorphodon*, had long tails to increase lift and help them steer. Later types, such as *Pteranodon*, were called pterodactyls. They had much bigger wings and tiny tails.

Did pterosaurs have feathers?

Most pterosaurs had furry not feathered bodies and their wings were made from sheets of leathery skin. In this way, they were more like bats than birds. The wings stretched from the pterosaur's body along its arm to the tips of its long fourth fingers. Their long wings were ideal for soaring on air currents.

Quick-fire Quiz

1. Which was the biggest pterosaur?
a) *Pteranodon*
b) *Quetzalcoatlus*
c) *Pterodaustro*

2. What were pterosaurs wings made of?
a) Feathers
b) Hair
c) Skin

3. What did most pterosaurs eat?
a) Fish
b) Dinosaurs
c) Insects

4. What were pterosaurs?
a) Dinosaurs
b) Reptiles
c) Birds

Death of the Dinosaurs

Dinosaurs died out about 65 million years ago. Studies show that they disappeared slowly in some places, but more suddenly in others. There are many theories to explain their death, but no-one knows for sure which is right.

Did a meteorite hit Earth?

One of the main theories is that a huge rock falling from outer space hit the Earth. This meteorite threw up a cloud of dust, blocking out the Sun's light and heat. The Earth became much colder and animals that could not cope with this died out. A huge crater that probably formed around this time has been found off the coast of Mexico. This evidence could mean that a meteorite caused the end of the dinosaurs.

Crater caused by a meteorite

United States

Gulf of Mexico

* Impact site

Did mammals eat dinosaur eggs?

One explanation for the death of the dinosaurs is that the number of small mammals increased. The mammals ate so many dinosaur eggs that few babies hatched. There are many strange theories and this is one of the more unlikely ones.

Did plant life change?

The extinction of dinosaurs and other animals may have been gradual. Towards the end of the dinosaur age, the tropical climate in North America became cooler and more seasonal and tropical plants were replaced by woodland plants. The dinosaurs seem to have migrated south, so perhaps they could not adapt to these changes in climate and plant life.

Did volcanoes make a difference?

Fossil plant remains suggest that by 65 million years ago the Earth's climate had become cooler. Some scientists think this was caused by several huge volcanic eruptions that took place over a period of half a million years. Volcanoes send up gases and dust that can first heat the atmosphere, then cool it down, killing off life.

Were there other mass extinctions?

The end of the dinosaurs was not the first mass extinction. About 440 million years ago almost half of the animal species died out, and again 370 million years ago. Over 95 per cent of all living things died out about 345 million years ago, and 210 million years ago, at the end of the Permian Period, many land vertebrates died out. When these events happen, new species can take over the world.

Survivors

Which animals died with the dinosaurs?

When the dinosaurs died out, so did many other reptiles, including mosasaurs, plesiosaurs, pliosaurs and pterosaurs. So did swimming shellfish like ammonites. Most other plants and animals, such as mammals, birds, frogs, fish and other kinds of shellfish survived. Not all reptiles died out either: turtles, crocodiles, snakes and lizards still exist today.

Timescale

The Earth formed about 4,600 million years ago and life developed about 1,000 million years later. The oldest known fossils, which are of shellfish, are 600 million years old. Dinosaurs arrived 230 million years ago and the first true humans about two million years ago.

First life: 3,500 million years ago

DEVONIAN

CARBONIFEROUS

When did dinosaurs live?

The dinosaur age, the Mesozoic Era, lasted from 250 to 65 million years ago. Scientists split this time into three main periods. Dinosaurs first appeared in the **Triassic**, about 230 million years ago. The continents were a single land mass called Pangaea ('All-Earth') and dinosaurs could roam all over the world at that time. During the **Jurassic**, about 145 million years ago, Europe and Africa began to move away from the Americas. In the **Cretaceous**, the land masses were separated and different dinosaurs developed on the different continents.

Triassic

Early Jurassic

Early Cretaceous

When did animals move on to land?

Life began in the sea. The first animals moved on to land about 380 million years ago. Amphibians like Eryops could breathe air but, like frogs and toads today, they had to return to water to lay their eggs and to keep their skin moist. Eryops was the size of a pig. Its thick skin protected it and helped support its body weight on land.

Eryops

Tadpoles

Reptile hatching

Which animals first lived on land?

Although amphibians could live on land they were not true land animals as they had to return to the water to breed. The tiny tadpoles that hatched had to stay in the water until they developed into adults. Reptiles were the first vertebrates (animals with backbones) that could live completely on land. They laid their leathery eggs on land and the baby developed inside the egg, feeding on the yolk. The newly hatched baby was fully formed and active.

CAMBRIAN

Fish evolve:
500 million
years ago

PRECAMBRIAN

When did fish develop?

The first fish swam in the seas about 500 million years ago. None of them had jaws or fins. Later fish like *Dunkleosteus* were huge predators. This armoured giant was 10 metres long and its jaws were lined with razor-sharp bony cutters for slicing up prey. It lived 370 million years ago.

Dunkleosteus

Modern times

Ornithomimus

TERTIARY

Cetiosaurus

CRETACEOUS

Hylonomus

PERMIAN   TRIASSIC   JURASSIC

Pentaceratops

The Mesozoic Era — the Age of the Dinosaurs

Eoraptor

Dimetrodon

Coelophysis

When did reptiles evolve?

Reptiles evolved about 320 million years ago. Early reptiles came in all shapes and sizes from the tiny *Hylonomus* at 20 centimetres long to 3 metres long *Dimetrodon*. One group of these early reptiles gave rise to the dinosaurs. Two of the earliest dinosaurs were *Eoraptor* and *Coelophysis*. Scientists think that another group of reptiles, called cynodonts, were the ancestors of mammals. Reptiles alive today include lizards, snakes, crocodiles, turtles and tortoises.

Quick-fire Quiz

1. What was the Age of Dinosaurs called?
a) Devonian
b) Mesozoic
c) Triassic

2. What was *Dunkleosteus*?
a) An amphibian
b) A reptile
c) A fish

3. What was the Triassic single land mass called?
a) Europe
b) Gondwana
c) Pangaea

4. What was *Dimetrodon*?
a) A dinosaur
b) A mammal-like reptile
c) An amphibian

After the Dinosaurs

After the dinosaurs died out, other animals developed to take their place. Warm-blooded mammals took over as the ruling animals. They dominated the land and even took to the air. A few even went to live in the place where life first developed – the sea.

What are the dinosaurs nearest surviving relatives?

Many scientists now agree that birds are the closest living relatives of the dinosaurs. The first fossil bird to be found was *Archaeopteryx*. It had a reptile-like skeleton similar to that of *Deinonychus* and feathered wings like a bird. *Archaeopteryx* had a long bony tail, three clawed fingers on each hand, and teeth. Modern birds have lost their teeth and their clawed wing fingers. Their small tail stumps hold their tail feathers.

Deinonychus

What were early birds like?

Very few fossils of early birds have been found. Several almost complete skeletons of *Hesperornis*, a diving bird that lived at the end of the dinosaur age, were found in the United States. *Hesperornis'* wings were so small that it was almost certainly flightless, but its large feet may have been webbed to help it swim. It looked much more like today's birds than *Archaeopteryx* but it still had teeth in its beak and a fairly long bony tail.

Why were mammals so successful?

There are several reasons. Early mammals had bigger brains and were more intelligent than reptiles. They were hairy and warm-blooded, so they could live in colder places. Most of them cared for their young for a long time, so perhaps more young survived. Also, different mammal groups had different kinds of teeth so they could feed on a huge range of food without competing with each other.

What were the first mammals like?

The first mammals evolved about 215 million years ago. One of the earliest known mammals is *Morganucodon*. This mouse-sized hunter was warm-blooded but probably laid eggs like the Australian platypus. *Zalambdalestes* lived at the same time as the last of the dinosaurs, and gave birth to live young.

Morganucodon

Smilodon

Zalambdalestes

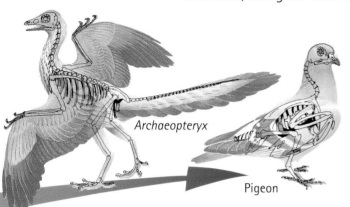
Archaeopteryx

Pigeon

When did mammoths die out?

The huge woolly mammoths died out about 10,000 years ago. The giant North American mammoth was as tall as a double-decker bus. These huge beasts were preyed on by *Smilodon*, a sabre-toothed cat with fangs as long as your hand (15 centimetres). When the mammoths died out, so did *Smilodon*.

Mammoths

Late arrivals?

The first humans evolved about two million years ago, but modern humans or *Homo sapiens* ('wise person') only arose about 100,000 years ago. In the Stone Age, 20,000 years ago, people lived in caves and hunted with stone tools.

Quick-fire Quiz

1. Which of these have no teeth?
   a) Birds today
   b) *Archaeopteryx*
   c) *Hesperornis*

2. Which was the earliest known mammal?
   a) *Mammoth*
   b) *Smilodon*
   c) *Morganucodon*

3. How long ago did modern humans evolve?
   a) 20,000 years
   b) 100,000 years
   c) 5,000,000 years

4. Which animals dominated after the dinosaurs?
   a) Mammoths
   b) Amphibians
   c) Mammals

Index

Quick-fire Quiz ANSWERS

Page 5 Digging up the Facts
1. b 2. c 3. c 4. b

Page 7 Colour and Camouflage
1. b 2. a 3. b 4. a

Page 9 Dinosaur Giants
1. c 2. a 3. a 4. c

Page 11 Small Dinosaurs
1. c 2. c 3. a 4. b

Page 13 Dinosaur Babies
1. b 2. a 3. c 4. b

Page 15 Communication
1. a 2. a 3. c 4. c

Page 17 Plant-Eaters
1. b 2. c 3. c 4. b

Page 19 Meat-Eaters
1. c 2. c 3. b 4. a

Page 21 The Fiercest Dinosaur
1. b 2. c 3. b 4. b

Page 23 Attack and Defence
1. a 2. b 3. b 4. c

Page 25 All Over the World
1. b 2. b 3. b 4. c

Page 27 Living in Herds
1. a 2. b 3. b 4. c

Page 29 Fast and Slow
1. b 2. b 3. b 4. c

Page 31 In the Sea
1. c 2. a 3. c 4. b

Page 33 In the Air
1. b 2. c 3. a 4. b

Page 35 Death of the Dinosaurs
1. c 2. a 3. b 4. b

Page 37 Timescale
1. b 2. c 3. c 4. b

Page 39 After the Dinosaurs
1. a 2. c 3. b 4. c